COME
WITH ME!

COME
WITH ME!

TERESA E. QUINLIN, M.D.

Halo
PUBLISHING
INTERNATIONAL

Halo Publishing International
7550 WIH-10 #800, PMB 2069,
San Antonio, TX 78229

First Edition, August 2024
ISBN: 978-1-63765-655-6
Library of Congress Control Number: 2024915047

Halo Publishing International is a self-publishing company that publishes adult fiction and non-fiction, children's literature, self-help, spiritual, and faith-based books. We continually strive to help authors reach their publishing goals and provide many different services that help them do so. We do not publish books that are deemed to be politically, religiously, or socially disrespectful, or books that are sexually provocative, including erotica. Halo reserves the right to refuse publication of any manuscript if it is deemed not to be in line with our principles. Do you have a book idea you would like us to consider publishing? Please visit www.halopublishing.com for more information.

For all who wish to explore life, purpose, and more.
For those who desire to open the heart and mind to enter in,
to win moments of peace and inspiration.

To feel Love!
Be Love!
See God!
In everyone!

Through pen and prose,
who knows,
where the journey will begin.
Art to inspire.
Words to point the direction, in this moment in time.
Come, read, feel, and unwind.

COME WITH ME!

Come with me,
Come journey inward to see,
inspirations and musings to inspire thee!

Come with me to see and believe in beauty.

Art, poetry, and hope to share.
Know that God, His Angels, and others care,
about you!

Open the pages to explore,
Love, hope, wellness, and more!

God lights the way, forever, and especially today!

CONTENTS

A Book is a Look

A book, is a look
into someone's knowledge
left to bare,

Their wisdom, their flair.
Is it history?
Is it a mystery?
A novel of sorts?
OR an epic course?

Does the book inspire,
or tire,
in the unfolding of its contents?
Is it uplifting
or is it drifting
off of its intended plan,
its intended course?

Does the book help one understand
The topic at hand?
Is it a masterpiece of knowledge,
of great worth?

Is reading it giving birth,
to the spirit and soul of (wo)man?
The great books can!
Illuminating us is a books plan!

Our time can be used to reveal,
in these great books,
those that have left their life's
journey,
their knowledge,
their work for others to read
and to take a deeper look.
Pick one up and find a cozy nook.

Read a good book!

A Day in July

A Day in July,
A year or two ago and it came
and went by.
This day started paving a way,
for me to begin to play
a *voice* of a different kind.

It would now allow me to say,
to give way,
To inspired ideas and such.
Thus, bringing calm to the day
Today's rush,
with thoughts and musings,
poems, with self and more
universal cruisings.

Taking on ideas and suggestions,
inspirations and sometime
posing questions.
Many directions and suggestions
flew through the air,
landing here, landing there.

Popping up during the night,
or by dawn's early light.
Sometimes a friend
speaks a word,
and off goes the flight
of the inspirational bird.

This colorful muse,
giving messages and clues.
Directing the course
the inspiration, no force.
For me, for you,
for the old and the new.

To fly above, bringing down
to earth,
a new poem to be birthed.
What inspires, what tires,
what brings hope,
if we are left hanging on
by the preverbally rope.

For you see,
God so inspires me.
Giving the direction
and most the time
the suggestions.
It is He who pens to thee!

My fingers glide
along the keyboard.
Sometimes so fast that He,
The Lord,
only can decipher the
hen-pecked jumble
of the typed keys!
Better to type, than write
so others can read, please!

Oh, please, I say, send the Heavenly
spellchecker my way!
So, the tale is now told
of how I have come to be so bold,
as to be prodded to share
this Heavenly inspired prose!

A Feeling of Trust, Hope Amongst us!

A feeling of trust,
amongst us.

A desire
that will not tire,
Even under adversity!
True hope, a necessity.

Hope Knows,
God shows,
His way,
Forever, even today.

Many have swayed,
from their hopeful
way.

Remind oneself, Hope is alive.
Hope wishes to thrive,
Inside.

Create Hope's place in one's mind.
One will find
their way
through the dark times that have
tried to steal the day.

Quiet the disquiet and uplift
the soul.
And know,
really Trust,
That God IS amongst us!

Hope is our power to love.
Be above,
Evil's gaze. Give God Praise.
raise Hope's power.

Faith has shown,
With God,
We are never alone!

What fear tries to steal,
be real to oneself. Be the Hope
and zeal
that Hope gives us to feel.

Trust, with Faith as its friend,
That Love
infused Hope will be with you
to Life's end!

Only God knows the way,
And is the one that knows the hour
and the day.

(*Dedicated to all those who have
been misled and told there is no
hope, you will be dead!)

A Good Dog

A Good dog
not only hears its Master's voice,
the Good dog obeys!
If only we,
could be,
so faithfully loyal and heed
to what we hear,
God's still small voice calling us
to be near.

A Good dog,
giving unconditional Love
and attention,
every nuance, look,
not wanting to forget to mention,
the look of love, with tail
a'wagging,
eyes sparkling,
ears moving in all directions.

Waiting to hear,
the Voice of the Master
so dear!
Come with me, and be,
enraptured with God's
masterful call.

That still small voice,
our choice
to see,
How HE loves and
cares for all,
especially you and me!

Let us be the Love the dog sees
in thee!
Let us be pleasing to God
and be forever Free!

A Hebrew Name
to Speak Out Loud

Ani Yahweh Ropheka
I Am God who Heals you,
is a wonderful Sacred Name
in Hebrew!
This sacred name,
came, from Aurora Adonai,
after a prayer request for healing
for several of my patients
and friends.

Use often, every day,
Pray.
Connect with God's presence,
call this into your mind and heart,
taking in its full essence.
Take part.
Be honest with yourself as a start.
What caused this all to start?

Then, my friend,
Send
the call,
use your will, surrender it all.

Be fully real
in your own healing,
through God.
Behave and do what is right,
and what is right
in front of you!

No cheating with Truth.
For truth will rise
to surprise,
turning the ignorant into
the wise.
The answers are within.

Begin, be brave, be loyal,
then with God,
be saved.
Saved from fear
and disease.

No cheating with Truth.
For truth will rise
to surprise,
turning the ignorant into
the wise.
The answers are within.

Begin, be brave, be loyal,
then with God,
be saved.
Saved from fear
and disease.

So, please, Remember,
We all are here under
God's dominion,
His Domain,
and will remain,
here, until our time is done.

So, come,
Come, chant these Holy Words,
knowing energy vibrations
will reverberate,
into tissues to help them begin
to exhilarate,
to regain their health and wealth.

Oh, this sacred word name,
Ani Yahweh Ropheka,
usher in healings to occur!
I am in, for sure.

A New Day

That's the way!
Get up and say,
"This is a fresh new day!
Let's be on our way!"

A Nightbird's Song for All

Nightbirds' song for all
A wake-up song call.
"It's ok, it's ok.
Come out and celebrate
the day."

No need to wait
to set a "happy" time or date.
even amongst dark times,
dark hours,
even in pain, causing one
to want to cower.

We can choose to be happy,
to be free.
Come, see.
These situations need
not define us.
Look inside and be the one
to choose,
to trust.
It's ok, it's ok, to feel lost.
"Everyone feels lost, at times.
Let it not define
your choice to be happy,"
Songbird sings.

Giving all a lift on her spiritual
song wings
Soaring above,
this, now, heavenly dove,
still inspires us
to inner trust.

Thank you for your life,
your song.
You have made it possible for us
to have hope and come along,
now knowing it's ok!
Be happy forever, starting today!

Soaring above,
this, now, heavenly dove,
still inspires us
to inner trust.

Thank you for your life, your song.
You have made it possible for us
to have hope and come along,
now knowing it's ok!
Be happy forever, starting today!

This poem was inspired by Jane (Nightbirde) Marczewski (1990-2022), an American singer-songwriter, who performed an original song "It's OK" on "America's Got Talent" while she was battling stage four cancer. She adopted the stage name Nitebirde due to a frequent dream in which birds sang outside her window at night anticipating morning. This reflected her positive attitude and her belief that, "You can't wait until life isn't hard anymore before you decide to be happy." Rest in Peace, Nightbirde!

A Note from a Friend

My friend, to the very end.
Through thick and thin,
we always win.

Joined together through
the bonds of love, friendship,
and grace,
we travel together, through time
and space,

Holding each other's hearts
in our hands, giving each other
a very sacred place.

A place to be,
delivered, to see,
we are loved and free!

Forever entwined by love's
plan divine,
we will forever be friends
throughout eternity and time!
To our friendship,
forever, I call you, My Friend.

Do you hear my spiritual phone?
Calling you, My Friend?
Oh, how Dear you are,
my special Friend!

A Star has been Born

A star has been born.
Shout and blow that
trumpeter horn.
You are a Super Nova, now.
WOW!

That's it!
You are in the groove.
Who knew!
That is what happened to me
last July,
for these words to take wing
and fly.

Bring your art out!
Let it shout,
as it will inspire others
to discover
what needs to be uncovered!

Cool!
Who knew?
You go, girl,
give it a whirl,
in this art endeavor.

How clever,
you are!
A STAR!

A Star that Reaches the Sky

A Star that reaches to the Sky,
Very hard to come by.
Why?

Some Stars are afar.
Some are only seen
while riding in the car.
Some are rising in the sky,
Others are falling nearby.
Others float by
in the sky
as the night goes by.

Others walk the earth,
Destined
by their birth,
To shine brightly,
Both daily and
nightly.

Their smiles,
Radiate into one's heart across
the miles.
Brilliant in their radiance,
their gift of love, life, their dance.
Amongst us they glow,
they flow,
In and out of our days
In ways
Only they can show.

So, when a Star crosses your
life path,
Ask them to stay,
to play
To let their laughter last.

Across the miles,
Bring out your smiles.
Give from yourself,
The gift
of the Star-crossed path,
nothing else.

That of comfort, joy, friendship,
and lifetime.
One will surely find,
Nothing more precious than
being kind.

So, let us be the Star
that reaches from the earth and
into the night sky!

Let's fully live before we die.
Let us be the brilliance,
of a Star,
one that flies deeply into
others' lives!
Let each of us go far!

Adopt Me, Please

Adopt me, PLEASE!
Comes the plea.
See in my eyes,
My inner cry,
For a forever home,
Never to roam,
Endlessly.

Looking for a home for me!
Can you open your heart?
Your door?
To give out more?
More of your love?

I am asking God from
above.
Home, home, oh, sweet
home,
there is grace, and space,
I have felt your heart race.
Is there a place for me
to be, free?

Free from the wonderings.
Am I cute enough?
Loveable enough?
Desirable enough?
Oh, I have tried to be so tough!

Maybe a cute smile,
after a while
will melt your heart.
So, no longer will you stall
to hear my heart's call!

Are there any words to say?
A style, a different way?
Should I wink my eye?
Smile or cry?
How about a hug?
Or a shoulder shrug?

How about MY LOVE?
Unconditional it will be,

Come see! Adopt me.
Please.
Whether the adoptee,
For thee,
Is a child born,
Not to be forlorn.
Or a four-legged friend,
Who will love you to the end.

Open the way
To say.
Home, sweet forever home,
Your home.

Automatic Reset

Automatic reset! What
a wonderful way,
to start a new day.
A beginning to an end,
to be well again!

Those past "mistakes"
whether one's own or another's
that has taken place.
Push that forgiveness button
from above,
if one cannot be
the freedom judge!
Let God help ease those heartfelt
pains and remorse.
and of course,
do what you have the power
to do!

That's the clue.
The Golden Rule.

So many illnesses take their hold,
when one's heart has turned
bitter and cold.
Let Go,
get into the Circle of Love flow.

Grievances have a tendency
to have molehills take one on a
mountainous ride.
Now, turn it around and glide!
Back to one's center, no longer
needing the illness to help
you hide.

The message was to wake
one up,
so as to be able to "arise"
and get up.
As from the Waters at Bethesda.
Let all jump into swim,
into health, into wealth, into
positivity
for all to see
how easy the reset can be.

Hit that reset button in those
memories that shackled one
to hate,
regrets and a dooming fate.
There is no health or wealth
for life to grow.
Goodness and kindness are the
ONLY way to go.

Many ways to help one recover.
Look more to natural,
God given wonders.
Seek answers from within.
Forgive yours and others' "sin."

Lots of modalities to aid if stuck.
Flower remedies, homeopathy,
hands-on healing and such.
Acupuncture, color and
sound therapies are a few more
in the mix—the bunch.

One most useful is
diaphragmatic breathing,
All leading
to help one to regain one's health.
Remember the first and last gift
God gives us is in the air.
So, take care!

Just Breath!
Breath in the Love, in the circle
of life.
Friends, sister, and brotherhoods
to share,
where everyone cares.
Breath out, what needs to go,
You know,
God is the ultimate recycler
of woes!

Now, the automatic restart button is
yours to use.
What good News!
Go and get rid of those ailing blues!

Aww, the Dentist!

Aww, the Dentist!
Is it a treat,
or is it a dental defeat?
Is that cavity worth drilling,
or does
the tooth need a pulling
or filling.

Is the smile sparkling clean?
Or do we need to be re-seen?
Brush, brush,
brush away every day,
keep those enamels clean,
for the dentist not to be seen.

Some are afraid to bare the teeth,
and be beneath,
the power of a dental drill!
Oh, what a thrill!
Some need anesthesia to be able
to bare the baring of one's teeth.

Is that a cavity way back there?
The dentist gives me that dental
mirror so I could inward stare.

What o' what do we gleam
from a smiling face?
Are all the teeth properly spaced?
If not, the orthodontist is next
in line.
Oh boy, watch those dollar signs!

Not one of my favorites,
unless to speak,
to open my mouth,
for the dentist to peek.
Then to give out a shout,
Aww, what is this all about???

So, if you are like me,
the dentist is not the one
I wish to see.
For him or her to explore
what next is in store!
Smiles.
Clean teeth,
that's what we aim for!

BAT BALLOON

Bat Balloon.
One that we will be seeing, soon!
Watch for it to fly high at night,
by the full moon.

Soon,
the Bat Balloon,
will be carrying wee ones,
that will be set free,
when ready,
on the by and by.

Free to fly
in the night sky.

Other bats have
already graduated,
and are nearby.
Already flying in this night sky.
Bat brothers, sisters, cousins,
and such,
in fact,
the whole clan came to see
this balloon
and make a fuss!

Giving encouragement, sharing
their hearts,
doing their part,
to encourage wee bats, who
are willing,
yet not able,
to be counted in the
"free me" label.

Under the grand care of
the Bat rescue crew,
always there to help.
This glorious Queensland crew,
knows what to do.

The bats, now out of Bat rehab,
have flown home!
The wee ones are being shown,
How to eat,
how to sleep,
how to tree top meet.

Then, off to their castle,
the cave, and others,
to their home,
waiting for another
perfect night to roam.

Bats be free! That will be soon!
But, until then, enjoy your ride
in the Bat Balloon!
Flying high during the full moon.

BE KIND

Be Kind and Pray.
This will lead the way.
And this will say,
A great way for all days!

Find the Time,
And Be Kind,
Find a way,
then start the day.

Be Kind in affection.
A step in the right direction!

The need is to turn attitudes
Into gratitudes.
A simple way to go.
Positivity is what we need
to know.
A smile will go a mile,
So, for just this while,
Ease someone's tribulation,
into jubilation.

Be Kind, it will show,
And it will grow,
Blossoming a Human Grace,
Help put someone's shame
in its place.

Be Kind,
And find
that Heart felt connection,
this, too, will point one in
the right direction!

Any chance
That you help another advance,
Is a kindness shown.
This reflects your inner state
of Love
in action.
Now watch their reaction!

A Joyous grin
Will reach their chin,

Pearls of laughter,
A state of rapture,
to witness Love,
begin.

All from a compassionate heart,
the start.
This can only be given,
Not driven!
So be Kind.

The Kindness you wish
to receive,
Then you will perceive,
Kindness all around,
The best to be found,
Has had its start,
coming from your
compassionate Heart!

What a way
To live the day,
Fully alive with Joy inside!
Oh, fill the Heart!

Now, feel the Circle of Love
come around.
Touching the mind,
the soul to find.
Its part to start the Kind actions
to be bound,
back to the Heart.

So that each day
In a perfect way,
Kindness will be King.
It will sing a new song,
A song of a compassionate being.

So come along,
Be Kindness in the doing,
Sing loud, sing long, sing a
melodious song.
A Child of God worthy
to sing the song of a
Kindness King!

Be Kind!

BEAUTIFUL DEBUSSY

Sing, sing,
Piano and violin string.

Talent extraordinaire,
David Oistrakh plays with
fluidity in the air!
Notes sing,
nay ring
from his bow and string.

Feel the passion,
enjoying talent that is honed
to perfection,
no question!

Debussy gifting us the notes,
the song score.
We cry "Play more!"
Let us begin to once again,
live and feel,
that which makes life
very special and very real!

BEAUTY AND GRACE

Beauty and Grace,
just presented its face,
through an artist's drawing
that was sent to my place.

Self-taught, and would like
to shout,
Oh My God,
What is this all about?
This beautiful flamingo bird
just appeared,
and it is unheard, that someone
had this hidden talent that
was just now birthed.

Flamingo, beauty, and grace,
was hidden inside, until one day
she ventured out,
never to hide.
Just look inside yourself,
to see what you are all about.

Let's all shout,
"Artists come out, be free,
be free,
be free, artist in me.
Let it all shine with God's
gift divine!"

Beauty and Grace, come out
and take your place,
Allow your life to take place
through art's grace.

Brisbane, Australia Bat Rescue

This fruit bat,
was rescued in Brisbane,
Australia.
Imagine that.

Named Donnie Darko,
what a charmer.
He needed love and to be fed,
and kept warmer.
Story has it that he needed
shelter and food to survive.

He was revived.
Bat rescuers to provide
all that he needed in
the shelter inside.
Donnie spied other bats there
as well.
Do tell.

When the others received
their meds,
food by syringe,
Donnie at first cringed.
Then decided that was his need.
Oh, God speed.

He wanted that special touch,
that handheld love from the
rescue bunch.
So, he now is grown, now
has flown,
off to find his bat tribe.
Wow, what a good vibe.

Rescuers, what cool gals
and guys!
Keep them all alive.

CALL ME HOME

For so long, I have been
wandering around,
walking and talking amongst
the earth bound.
For so long, I have been lost,
and now found.

The flute whistles, and sings
through the trees,
gleaming and singing notes
of joy and laughter,
freeing one.

Oh, let us forever be Free!

The Harp plays along,
singing of the rising sun,
giving us a heartfelt feeling
of being One!

Give glory to Jesus, the firstborn,
the Risen Son!

Lift me, oh God, into your bliss,
give me your heavenly kiss.

No longer do I wish to miss,
Your love delivered to me,
from above.

Call me home, call me home!

The Angels are here to assist.
No longer do I resist,
the call home to live amongst
your Heavenly Bliss!

Hearing the Angelic joyful call,
You have sent them to grace all.

Let us turn our eyes around.
Now, no longer lost, we are
joyfully found.

Here we are now residing and
abiding in your loving embrace.

Thank you, thank you, for your
songs, and Your Blissful
Grace.

No words can express, the feeling
one will find.
Our life of love now eternally
entwined!

Oh, how we are so blessed to be
called home!

CANCER ANSWER

Cancer answer-
Is—I Can Sir!

I can answer,
With my Inner power
and might,
This isn't the route,
Let us shout—
I will overcome with the
good fight.

See the outcome you wish to be,
Take the inner visual journey
with me.
Look inside, what is there to hide?

Grief, pain,
An unresolved fortune
not gained?
Anger, grief, lost love?
Something else, something not
received from ABOVE?

Has the diet been pure,
Look to be sure!
Healthy nutrition
Is another addition!

What about sugar and
other addictions?
Let Go!
Let Go!
Get into the positive flow.

No worries or concerns
are worth dying over,
Unless one wishes to be living under
the grass and four-leaf clovers.

To see the inner health is
the main key.
Pairing the health inner vision
with emotion
will bring it to reality.
See how the end result is to be.

Feel it,
See it,
Be it.
Dance the inner joy of it.
Sing it, internally.

Become alive for the vision
to be set free.
Breathe deep and breathe wide.
Cancer cannot hide.
It's the fact that our health and
healthy ways have been asleep.

Awake, oh awake,
It's NEVER too late,
Let us accomplish
the healthy feat!
I Am awake!!!
Now, to my healthy state.

Wait,
Feel this blessed state
in our mind, body, and soul,
as our permanent fate,
One, that we create.

Our thoughts bring our reality,
Look in the mirror to see,
What reality are you creating
for thee?

Neville Goddard's Book on Prayer,
"The Art of Believing"
Is a book worth receiving!
Inside,
Is a guide,
To bring about,
The change in inner
thinking route.

Awaken now and be about,
Health, vitality, and then shout,
"I Can, Sir,
be free of cancer."

A sleeping, lower vibrational
health state
is now Awake!
Joyfully celebrate
another day.

Let's Play!

CATCH A BUTTERFLY

Catch a Butterfly,
whisper a wish, then let it fly.
Say hello,
then goodbye!
Up to the heavens it will go,
releasing the wish to bless
all below.

Spirit wings they fly by.
Lifting, soaring, and fluttering
in the sky.
Blue, yellow,
monarchs, and such,
just give them
your whispered wish, quietly,
a hush.

Release them with a gentle touch.
The Butterfly soaring upward
in the sky,
carrying our wish
ever so high.
Is it a wish for Love? To fulfill
a dream?
Is it for health, wealth, wisdom,
or for forgiveness,

Or something else to fulfill
the wish, it seems?
Send those fulfilling wishes
to those near and far,
Butterfly wishes fulfilled
will be soaring
back to us, from the stars!
Nothing too big
or too small, the Butterfly
carries them all!

So gently let the Butterfly
come to you!
Sitting on your shoulder,
very close to you!
Their magic now entwined
with the wish!

Give the Butterfly your playful
wish list!
Off now to soar, to explore,
all the possibilities at hand,
Your wish, now, is their command!

CATCH ME IF YOU CAN

Catch me if you can,
said the wind, as it ran across
the land.

The rain then spoke and said,
"You are just smoke,
blowing hither and yon,
be quiet, be gone!"

"You see, Mr. Smoke,
I put out forest fires,
Nourish the rivers and land,
I can go near and far!
I am a Super Star".

"Not so fast, Miss Rain, "
the wind came to say,
I can blow you and
the rain clouds
around if I may.
Everyday!"
Just watch me play!"

Then Mother Earth spoke
out loud,
"Who are you to speak,
Wind and Rain,"
What do you have to lose or gain?"
Mother Earth with a Voice
of Power, being very loud.

"With my magnetic earth spin,
surely this is where it all begins!"
God created the Firmament,
before Rain
and Wind!"

"I cause the Swirling of the Oceans,
the height, the majesty
of the Mountains,
and bring forth the fertile land.
Come to my Wisdom, come all
to understand.
This is where the wheel of life
enters in.

This is where the real
motion begins.
Thus, giving you, Wind,
and Rain, a place to play,
frolic, and spin!"

"Whoa, just a minute," speaks
the Sun.
Where is all of this coming from?
Are you all just kidding, having
some fun?"

"If there was no Sun Spark,
to ignite,
there would be no life.
Just barren soil, hunger,
and strife."

"No life without Light to bring
forth the day.
For all to grow, eat, and play."

"Colors burst forth from
my Radiant beams.
Colors of all varieties
can be seen."

The rainbow will play across
the sky,
touching both the Earth,
the clouds, the sky.
All can see the joining of the Wind
and Rain with these Sun beams.
So it seems,
that all must be together to have
perfect life and weather."

Then a Voice loud and clear,
suddenly appears.

"My, children all so dear,
do not Fear.
There is room for all,
each to call,
your special gifts to display."

"Each of you is needed to bring
forth life, to love, to play.
Be of good cheer,
as I created all, you dears.
Now, go off to play,
be at Peace, remember to Pray."

So says God to each of His children
created for His Eternal day.

Catch the Wind

Catch the wind,
"Let us begin!"
The Captain bellows
to his sailors,
with a grin.

"There's water below,
wind in the air,
let us set sail to who
knows where!"

"The journey across the sea,
that is very pleasing to me!"

"Now, come about,"
he says with a shout.

"Duck your heads as the boom
swings by,
otherwise, you'll be in the sea
looking up at the sky."

"The wind is strong today,
this ship is ready to play.
Unfurl those sails, so off we go,
only the wind knows where
it will blow."

Others, too, take notice
of this prize in the sky.
They, too, have their spirits high.

Now, here's the wee one
with a kite in hand.
Tying a long tail and string
to let his kite sing.
What joy will this bring,
Running against the wind
across the land,
he will see,
his kite above the trees.

Up, up and away it goes.
Gleefully digging in his feet
and toes.
The wind is strong today.
Joyous time to be outside
and play.

Look how high in the sky
the kite goes as it is lifted
and flies.
Up to the clouds as they drift by.

Another wee one has a helium
filled balloon.
Celebrating a birthday,
and soon,
will let it go to watch the wind
carry it away.
Grinning and smiling as if to say,
happiness is fun, so let's
enjoy today!

Others, too, like to catch
the wind.
The wind surfer stands
on the water to begin!
Capturing just the right wave
and angle on his board,
off he goes, bouncing and turning,
and soaring, and more.

Some sit in a basket powered
by hot air.
Lilting into the sky without
a care.
They catch the wind at the dawn
of the day.
Lifting, drifting, across the horizon
for miles at a time.
Only to find,
the wind is the master this time.

The most daring are those who
jump out of planes,
catching the wind on their way
down to the ground.
Needless to say, the wind must
be caught that day!
Otherwise they will make
a loud sound!
That is their way to play!

Wind chimes too come to mind.
Singing with the wind, playing
musical note rhymes.

Birds in the air,
catch the wind without care.

Butterflies are lifted high,
fluttering gracefully as the wind
carries them by.

Not to forget the cloud people
high above in the sky.
Waving and portraying their
love of the Wind Guy.

Waving flags also to share,
that the wind is there!

Together, all share,
the love of the wind blowing
in their hair.

Remember the next time one
is out and about,
feel the wind on one's face
and give an appreciative shout.

"Thank you wind for allowing
one to feel,
another gift from God to make
life fun and real."

Chocolate Roar

Chocolate roar!
Must I say more?
More chocolate
Or?

Or what?
You do not know?
Have you not lived?
Not embraced the day?
Let me just say—
Chocolate lives forever more!

Deliciously exploring
Those delightful receptors
that refuse all ignoring
of a rational approach,
Trying to coach
us away from the pantry door!

Make way for chocolate,
comes the roar!
Whether it be a chocolate
flourless torte,
And we all report,
No better way
To end our day,
Then with that chocolate
infused raptured state,
Cleaning every morsel off
our plate.

That chocolate grin
Is sure to win,
A five-star rating
for the baker who is making,
These delectable treats.
Boy, is she sweet!

From her OMG cake,
To the chocolate chip (GF)
cookies she makes.
I hear the next masterpiece.
Will be Another Day's
creative feat!
Do you hear that distant
chocolate roar?
It's saying, please bring more!

Cougar Power

Cougar power is of this hour.
Standing as a Queen,
soon to be seen
With a forest crown upon
her head.
Do not dread!

She walks both with power
and grace,
serenity across her beloved face.

Largest cat of her race.
She is ready to go with a fast
running pace.

Nestled between Birch
and Aspen trees,
blending both the rustling
of the leaves of the Aspen tree,
and the roots of the Birch tree,
she is hiding beneath their leaves.

Mother to her cubs is her most
excellent role.
Just stay away from her teeth
and sharp claw toes!

When the leaves of the Aspen
dance in the wind,
that is when she hunts, following
the scent to begin.
Hunting to feed her cubs is her
role to fulfill each day.
Then watch the cubs as they
gleefully play.

In her hunting with her
honed skills,
She watches all with her
keen eyes,
ready and waiting to see
her prize.

What an enormous thrill.
To see and watch and engage
in this hunt for life to survive,
she sacrifices for her cubs
to thrive.

This reigning Queen is a
wonderous sight to behold.
Gentle, yet fierce, she can be
very bold.
She sees us before we see her,
we are told.

So, when in the forest where she
lives today,
be watchful and alert as one may
become her dinner prey!

Dance with Me

Dance with me!
Come alive, be set free!

Flowing out to center stage,
to display,
the inner you and the inner me.

Colors surround,
and abound,
swirling around,
to embrace the inner
you and me!

Can you see the joy
and feel free?
Scarves around yours
and my wrists,
give a dancing twist.

One that cannot resist,
the swirl in the movement
of the dance quest.
There is no need to rest!
Just enjoy, give it your best!

Music now playing,
adds graceful notes to the swaying.
The feet tapping, moving,
and playing to an inner beat.

Beat, beat, the heart thrums,
listening to the beat, beat,
beat of the drums.

Guitar strums,
also engaging in the fun.
Now, the invitation for one to clap,
and to slap
the knees, or hum.

Choose a rhythm, one's own
inner tune.
Just have fun.
See the colors come alive.
Come join me on stage,
in this dancing vibe.

Come, dance with me!

Departures

Departures come,
some slowly, others run,
to journey the last leg of
their race,
leaving the earth, for our
heavenly space.

Some prepared,
others scared.
Some joyfully await
their open door at
the Pearly Gate.

Know that all will someday
this journey to be.
Are we each prepared to see,
that which awaits us at this Gate?
Prepare now,
before our final Earthly bow.
Be pleasantly surprised,
for all God's Glory that
He supplies.

Lift one's life now to him,
Just begin,
to prepare your space,
Be led by God's Grace.
There is still time,
to completely fulfill God's design,
for one to find,
His Mercy and His Grace.

He so much wants us
to be embraced!
Taking our earned place,
by His side.
Angels now with tears of joy abide,
dwelling in choices on earth
that were well applied.

Enter in stride,
through the open Gate doors.
Now in Heaven for one to live,
love, laugh, and explore.
See all that wonders now in store!

So, departure time,
coming closer each minute,
in each day,
Just be prepared.

Forgive, do good,
love, help others,
Get in God's woman and man's
sister-brotherhood.

Our Savior has prepared our way,
Be thankful, receive and say,
I wish to be united
with You, someday!

So, when our time clock rings
the time to depart,
Jump up, to sail, fly, or train
ride to start,
God's Love journey back
to His bosom,
His Heart.

Returning to the source of Love,
now fulfilling our part,
Becoming a vessel of true,
unconditional Love to everyone,
A Godchild of Love from the start!

Dinner Delight

Dinner delight,
tonight, and all days.
Was found and sampled tonight.
The feasting is such
a culinary delight!

Nicely displayed,
and laid,
for one to eat.
What a treat.
A cook, nay say,
A chef, here to play!

Combining herbs and flavors,
Everyone clamoring to savor.
No formal skills from some
fancy school,
just learned skill,
His was perfected by
the writings of
pen and quill.

Mother's recipes are at
the top the list,
the best of the bunch!
Hurry up, display your skills,
we are a hungry bunch,
waiting to munch.
Isn't it time for lunch?

Ring that dinner bell!
Oh, do tell,
what is in store?
For us to explore.
Then comes Robuchon's
masterpiece, his recipe book.
Or another favored one,
if one cares to look,
is the Joy of Cooking book.

To sweeten, yet, the culinary pot,
Add Julia Child's beef
bourguignon recipe, eat it hot!
Then Betty Crocker is not to
be out done
For simple and pleasing favorites
and fun!

Say Grace before each meal,
God appreciates our
acknowledgement, praise,
and zeal!
Thank the chef, the plants,
and the food-fare.

All to bring nourishment,
and loving care.
To us from another's skill
and touch.
Thank you, Chef,
Oh, so very much!

Remember to wash one's hands
Before the meal.
Clean your plate with zeal.
Then save room for a delightful
dessert or some sweets or cheese,
to please.

Signaling the end of a
wonderful meal!
Help the chef and or host,
With a thankful toast!
No limit to the boast of the man
behind the toast,
The skill he has revealed
In yet another memorable meal.

DO THE HULA-HOOP GROOVIN' MOOOVES!

A phrase,
Not praise,
Sent to me
With a plea!
"OMG, I am shaking in
my booooooots.

You two, putting your noggins
together, terrifies me no end!
Please send me or be a friend!
So, the friend sends,
A reply, cry,

Ends tied together makes a circle.
Close the loop.
Jump into it and do the hula -hoop.
Swing those hips,
do not trip!

Kick up those hula boots!
No more shakn'
And no more quakin',
You are just makin',
The hula-hoop hip-hop grooves!
Get those boots on the mooove!"

DOCTOR, DOCTOR, HEAL ME QUICK!

"Doctor, Doctor, heal me quick!
Give me the *quick fix!*"

"No matter what the cause,
Do not pause,
send me away,
Rx in hand to placate me, I say!"

"No matter if the diagnosis
is simple or grim,
Give me something—I'm out
here on a limb!
No need to investigate,
that may take time,
I won't change anything
that you may find.
In a bubble I have lived,
Letting life flow through
me like a sieve!"

"Forgetting that the place
I am now in,
Has followed alongside me and
the problem born from within."

"Instead of Wisdom and Grace,
Let me stay on and on,
in my current rat race.
Keeping pace,
With the habits that bring harm!
I have yet to hear the sounding
of the health alarm!"

"Doctor, Doctor what are you
trying to say?
I MUST change my way?
Do or die?
You say, I am saying goodbye?"
"No quick fix?

No more tricks?
Stay here and change
the way I play?
And I must change today?"

"I now need to pay the piper
for the years spent,
Trying to buy everything
and still pay the rent.
Where is the Joy,
In all these sought after toys?"

"Now, reckoning is at hand.
What? I need a new plan?
Oh my,
I am beginning to understand!"
Wisdom and inner Joy,
Brings health to this boy!

Get the nutcracker out to crack
those habits of old.
They are not your treasure
of silver or gold!
The only measure
Of your health, your treasure,
Is the Peace in your soul.
"Doctor, please help me so!"

"Help me find once again,
the sparkle in my eyes.
What youth gave me in a full
measured supply!"
"The laughter and jokes
we used to tell,
made us smile and our hearts
to swell.
With mirth!
Not an expanding
abdominal girth!"

"Let my vitality now flow
through me, down to my toes.
Let life flow!
Show me the way I need to go!
Do not delay!
Help me find myself today!"

"Doctor, Doctor, the Rx I need
Is the wisdom to see!
The courage to go,
The knowledge to show,
The new path of life in which
to grow!"

DRAGON FIRE

Dragon fire may impart,
fear from the start.
The lore,
and more,
that surrounds the tales,
telling of Dragon wings
and Dragon scales.

How Dragons can impart,
fear in all hearts.

Their Dragon flights,
their Dragon plights,
into human affairs,
that are meant to scare,
to control everyone below.

Their winged flights in the sky,
coming from a distance,
by and by.
Many a dragon story, from many
medieval folks,
speak of the Dragon, as a friend,
no joke!

However, a maiden fair,
is here to share,
how to overcome the plight,
of the fire-enraged
Dragon's plight.

For you see, the demon to be,
is a heart that's
not free.
Never having found love.

Never having a loving
touch from above,
has left the Dragon's heart
and soul,
burning, embers aglow.

Rage and the Dragon's own fear,
not allowing anyone near.
Until the maiden fair,
overcomes her fears and begins
to care,
for the beast entrapped within
the Dragon's body and soul.

This care and love then grows,
this maiden's wisdom
of love sows,
a soothing embrace,
a kiss to the Dragon's fierce face,
caressing with Love's grace,
bringing a touch of kindness to the
Dragon's fiery glare.

Eyes no longer needing to stare.
A wink,
a gentle blink,
cross the fiery one's face.

His countenance
no longer ready to pounce,
Gently relaxing and wanting
to be touched,
by Love's embrace.

Now, feeling the Grace.
Soon, the Fire of the Demon leaves,
Arising from the touch of care,
of Love now being there.

The Dragon's Fire,
now a Love's desire,
is here and forever to inspire,
all to rise above the lore
to explore,
A dragon's tale of Love,
and more.

This is how to tame
an internal flame,
to birth wings to soar into
a life filled with
peace, joy, deep into the heart
of the Dragon's lore.
Love, here now, and ever more.
Open Love's Dragon Door!

Easter Baskets and Floppy Easter Bunny Ears

No tears unless one gets up late
to the Easter Egg Hunting
and the chocolates bunnies left
on the Easter plates.
Jellybeans of many flavors,
to savor.

Each color and hue,
a different delectable flavor
to choose.
Some like the red,
others are led,
to the black licorice bean.

Many like the marshmallow
chickens, sprinkled with sugar,
no cream.

Unless it's inside a Cadbury
chocolate egg!
Everyone begs,
"Give me a Cadbury egg!"

Some prefer the dark
chocolate rabbit,
wanting to break the tradition,
the habit.
of which part
to start
to eat,
of this delectable chocolate treat.

Ears first, the foot, the ear, or tail?
Always an event,
to present,
chocolate rabbit for the first bite
to delight, that Easter
Bunny chocolate
zeal.

To finish off the fun,
is to run,
and find,
all the hidden, decorated,
and colorful Easter eggs.
Don't be left behind!

Bring that Easter basket,
now filled to the brim,
to showcase all the findings within!

So, closely this Easter day
is approaching,
to celebrate Easter's
traditions.
All now to focus on the Christian
nature of this inspired event.

God wished us to celebrate
His gift of
His Resurrected Son!
Now, go have Easter Fun!

Easter Honey Bunny Miracle

Easter Honey Bunny miracle
came about today.

A young girl prayed and prayed.
"Dear Saint Anthony
 help me find,
My bunny, named Peanut,
if you would be so kind.
Saint Anthony you see,
the Bunny hopped away from me."

"An escape artist, Peanut,
has become,
Jumping over the cage and
going out for a hop and run.
There are dangers a foot."

"Nightfall to come,
Saint Anthony help Bunny run
back into my arms, my loving
embrace,
Peanut, through God's Grace."

"Saint Anthony, Tony, if I may say,
is God's source,
of course,
to bring back what's been lost,
Waiting to turn around,
to be found,
to restore one's faith,
that miracles do take place!"

So, the Bunny tale enfolds,
Prayers being sent to unload,
this young girl's heart,
filled with Love gold.
A delivery man first spies,
Honey Bunny huddled by a door.
Oh, he sees this Bunny needs
help and more!

He knocks on Sara's door,
hoping that she can explore,
the need for this Bunny to have
a home.

Not to roam!
Sara, a kindhearted lass,
helps Honey Bunny
to find a repast.

Soon flyers are spotted
around the town,
"Heh, look Honey Bunny,
I believe
I have found,
your forever friend and home,
Come, let's text and phone."
Sara exclaims!
This will help ease the child's
emotional pain.

Soon the connection was made!
Honey Bunny now claimed,
Peanut is his real name.

Others helped to bring about
this Easter Miracle
and delight.
Thanks to all who aided
in this Easter Bunny reunite.
A miracle received tonight!

God speed to all!
Remember to always give Saint
Anthony a personal call.
He is happy to aid one and all!
When looking for the lost,
he's the boss!

Thank you, delivery man,
for your kindness and care,
For Bunny to land in Sara's
domain and home so fair.
Thank you, Chuck, to provide
your expertise and aid in the care,
of Honey Bunny's needs,
bringing food and cage for Bunny's
lettuce leaves.

Thank you (relative friend) for the
posting of the flyers around town,
to capture the attention of those
looking for Bunny to be found.

Everyone under the prayer!
See, there are many who care!
Another Miracle to share!
Loving care
all around town!

ENTERING THE ABODE

Entering the Abode,
Kick up one's feet, take off
the day's weariness and load.

Get comfortable,
Stay awhile in this place.
Give time to reconnect,
Get into God's grace.

Enjoy a hot meal,
reconnect with one's family,
the real deal.
Turn off the electronics,
T.V. and more.
Take the time and explore,
what the day had in store.

Give gratitude for all the
blessings this day gave.
What promises were fulfilled
and allowed you to play,
God's game of hide and seek.
Take a peek,
into the game of loving life.

Do so before the day's done
and it's turned into night.
Get outside, see God's nature
and His Glory.
See the sun, then moon, then stars,
to end the day's story.
Now off to bed,
Bible stories to be shared and read.

Seeking first God's kingdom
at hand,
then extend one's spirit to listen,
then land,
to hear God's eternal
life-giving plan.

Now, night has arrived,
sitting with us by our side,
the ticking of the clock,
will help us take stock,
of how blessed we are to
understand,
God's promise and care,
for each of us,
all in His Divine plan.

EVERLASTING LOVE

You've got to love Jeremiah!!!

Chapter and verse!
For what it is worth:
A Bible's blessing,
Addressing:
" I will love you with an
everlasting love."

God's promise,
Lifting any curse.
So, you say,
Have it your way.

Today!
And always!

Just have fun and play, play,
play!
God is here to say:
Have it My way!
Everlasting Love
Is above,
All forms of play.

Rest in My embrace,
My Grace,
Then Go play!
Eternity is now and forever
in a day.

Eye of the Storm, Dare to Dream

Eye of the storm, dare to dream,
The possibilities so far unseen.
The secret foretold
by Einstein himself,
Nothing is permanent
and on a shelf.

What one believes can be real,
Just dream and feel,
The real deal.
Calmness is in the Eye of
the storm,
Ever around us,
Yet we will not be torn!

Dare to dream,
Even within a storm.

Our hearts and our minds
Will pave the energetic way
to find
That $E=mc^2$ is the energy to bind
Our reality and creativity.

Energy= mass(matter)
to the speed of light,
The constant that never
takes flight.
Illuminating,
Relating,
The magnetic, energetic way,
To say,
Nothing is ever lost.

Einstein's way,
the Boss.
Happiness untold
Will unfold,
As we unload,
Our worries and cares,

As we thought compare
To be governed by God's
universal energetic plan,

We draw unto ourselves
and land,
Exactly according to this inner
state of being.

Synchronicities and Divine
timing then start freeing,
The old worn out scheme.
And melt into a new life stream.
That of co-creating one's life,
No longer a victim in our
self-imposed strife.

So, join in the knowing,
That God is bestowing,
His Love and free will choice to
each of
us.

Get the Secret out,
Do shout,
"I believe in goodness and His
Divine plan.

I now take my stand,
Freedom from worries and
fears,
I live life, fully, endeared,
That both our Earthly Life,
and Eternal Life is Good
and in God's Plan!"

Faith is a Place

Faith is a place
of power in God's grace.
The assurance of things
hoped for,
Prayer sent to Heaven's door.
The conviction of the answer
yet seen,
Arriving on time at the scene!

Not wavering a bit in asking,
Knowing that one prayer is
everlasting.
Hearing and believing
in the Word,
given to us,
Allows us to trust,

That trials, tribulations,
delays in the perceived results,
Is a way to build the Faithful
spirit, free of earthly insults.

Trust is a bold confidence,
inner security.
It's what one does because
of that inner surety.

Faith, the God given gift,
Is the navigator to give our
soul a lift.
To exercise the faith gift
given to us,
That's the role of
inner trust.

So, when I am asked to pray,
Yesterday or today,
My faith allows the deep connection,
To give my prayer that direction,
To connect in a way
To say,
"Blessings come forth
from Your Love,
Help us (me) from above!"

"Already both You (God) and
I know,
That you allow our faith to grow,

By the asking, the prayer
to show.
That Love connection."

Ask only in prayer once,
the truly Faithful know.
No more is ever needed,
that is how inner faith grows.

More prayers requesting the same,
It's a spiritual shame.
Showing doubt in one's
"connecting" abilities!
Making us beggars on our knees.

As God's children and Chosen ones,
We are daughters and
His sons.
No beggars are we to be,
Rise up off those faithless
knees!

Praise God for the Blessings given.
Have trust, build one's faith,
get spiritually driven,
Celebrate our Divine connection.
Faith is our God given direction!

Faith is the place,
God is the Grace!

Fear Tears

Fear tears, say no more!
Goodness and light
are here to restore.
Where shadows lay,
there is light to say,
Joy is the way today.

Fear is of the mind,
not to intertwine with the love
in the heart.
Keep them separate and apart.
Cast the fear upon the wind.

Begin to see, there is no reality.
Mind stuff, trying to puff,
a design of some kind,
to hold one back.

To suppress,
and depress,
a journey forward.
Into uncharted domains.

So, remain, calm, centered,
and reenter,
the peace in knowing,
that God and Angels will forever
be showing,

One's next natural progression,
in and through those fear
mongering
mind sessions.

One can also use a lift,
out of the fear blues.
Many can read the automatic
reset news!
There is always a hidden way,
waiting to say,
"Come here my dear.

No further need for anxiety,
fear.
God Loves you, my dear!"

"No harm,
just blessed love charm.
Plenty for all each and every
day."

"Come, my dear, come this way!
Wipe away those
fear tears!"

FILLED WITH JOY

I am Filled with much Joy.
Sending you some,
Allow yourself abundant fun!

Just heard from a friend,
Mercury retrogrades soon
to end!

Energy now ready to spin,
Clockwise,
no more disguise,
allowing bigger grins
to free the space
everywhere, every place.

Grins galore
No more hidden plots and ploys,
harmony being restored!

Soak up the joy,
be ye girl or boy,
there's more in store!
The love abounds.
Shouting its loud sounds!

Joy today!
Come out with me to play!

For All That You Are, All That You Do

For all that you are,
and all that you do,
This note is a reminder to you!
Who you are
is noticed from afar!

Praises are being sung out loud,
informing those near
and those that are amongst
the crowd.
The ones who
also have noticed how dear,
How you reach out and help
those far and near.

Whether by a helping hand,
Taking a righteous stand,
Donating of one's essence,
Or the giving of monetary
presence.
Most of all, it's the unconditional
love and care,
It's the counting on
that you will be there.

It is comforting in the knowing,
whether high waters are a flowing,
or winds a blowing,
There you are with love showing.
Purposefully filling the edict of
service
to others in need,
Everyone notices
and takes heed.

Here is God's helping hand,
Walking and talking giving of self,
of love throughout the land.
For all that you are,
and all that you do,
We thank you!

Forever in a Day

What did I just say?
Forever is today.
God is eternally present.
He sent,
this gift to us.
Want to discuss?

Let's think,
and in a blink
the Power is here,
to be very clear.
Our past, our present,
and our future
is oh, so near.

So close, there should be no fear.
All three
are the immediate reflection
of thee.
What has happened, the past,
went by so fast.

Today is ok.
It is here to lay,
the present as a gift,
for us to shift
and not drift
into decay!

Forever is IN a day.
The future is made from those
two.
Therefore, nothing is new.
What you do,
is already the future for you.

Change the present, especially
one's attitude.
The future then is already
created by you,
Now fill it with goodness and
gratitude!
God is present Now.
WOW!

All three in one,
And we are His daughters and
sons.
Forever present with God
in His created Eternal Now!

Therefore,
No more,
is there any doubt.
Your influence in the now,
is what one is all about.

Pay attention!
Every thought, every direction,
and in every second.
One calls and beckons.
One's future to be alive now,
that's the spiritual lesson.
You are your own invention!

Tomorrow is today!
Forever is now,
there is no delay!
All healing, all wealth,
All thoughts of a perfected self.
Are here now, our eternal treasure.
Stored before us as the gift of the
Present.

Use one's key of enlightened
thought,
and be brought,
To your immediate gift,
the Present.
Forever IN today.

FORGIVENESS, FORGIVENESS, FORGIVENESS

Forgiveness, Forgiveness,
Forgiveness,
That is what needs to be present,
to be Blessed,
for you, for me, for all of us!

Give, receive, all there to please.
Clear the air of that which needs
to be
surrounded with Loving care.

Yom Kippur, for sure, is now
upon us,
and as such, a time of
Atonement, attunement,
Like lent,
a time to repent.

Eternity of peace, time well spent.
Be the Beautiful tone,
in Atonement!
Be at Peace, in the moment.
Reflect, make amends,
no more inner or outer enemies,
just friends.
Fast and pray, forever say,
forgive and be forgiven,
directly sent to us from Heaven.

GOD SPARKS

God sparks,
here to show,
what embers glow,
inside us for us to know,
His light, His Love, His direction,
from above.

Embers breathed into our life,
some from joy, some from strife.
All to gather us to Him
so we can begin,
a Soul journey within.

Looking and seeking that will
bring the embers alive,
helping each of us thrive,
from our spiritual side.
Distractions a many,
can come our way,
just say,
"I am here for God today."

Keep those sparkling
embers aglow!
Seek God to know,
which way and choice to go.
Clean the cobwebs of stuck
thoughts,
get rid of those that do
not serve God
and us!

Trust!

That's God's way.
It may not look perfect today,
know that His Love leads us
in God's Perfect way.

His Sparks,
His Inspirations hit the mark.
Perfect in the end,
God and Jesus, our Eternal friend!

HAZEL'S HAVEN

Hazel's Haven is a place,
just around the corner,
a sacred space.

Flowers in the corner garden
of Tracee's home
where friends and family come
to gather to share and care,
walk about, or just wonder
and roam.

Hazel's memories linger
in each heart,
she being the matriarch.

Hazels' Haven is a beauty
to behold!
Family, friends, and neighbor's
we are told,
come often to experience this place
of wonder and beauty, and peace.
Everyone likes to take their shoes
off so the ground and grass can
tickle their feet!

There is a recycled treasure
from the neighbor's trash,
and in a flash,
an old bunkbed ladder leans
against the side of the house wall,
holding plants, flowerpots, and
flowering vines, now growing tall.

Tracee's garden, now an area
of joy and peace, giving
a grounding spot
for one to release, cares
and worries, sharing thoughts
of the future to joyfully unfold.
All are welcome, young and old.

The children with their inner
curiosity, they come to see
the bugs, flowers, and the bees!
Hazel would be so pleased!
"To gather and not scatter,
to share and care for each other.
Friends, family, sisters,
and brothers."
That's the words of her
wisdom peace.

Never goodbye, it's just until
we meet again.
Heaven-ward is now
Hazel's home!

"Come visit me soon, my friend,"
Hazel would say.
"Come and visit, sit a spell,
and stay."

"Come to my Garden,
my Haven of joy and peace."
"Let me ease your burdens,
give them a rest, God will
take care of you,
all you must do is just be
and do your very best!"

So next time there's a worry
too hard to bear,
give it to Hazel, a Dear Heart,
one who will forever care!

HEARTS TO YOU

A very wise Rabbi has come
to show,
what our Hearts already know.
Faith is the power to grow.
Not a dead branch, limp
and fragile,
clinging to an unknown power.

Faith comes to us at our
darkest hour.
Faith being built in each
of us each minute and hour,
like a bud opening,
ready to flower.
The scent of the heart
is of roses,
to start.

Heavenly healing for hearts
that may be torn.
In the pilgrimage comes first
the thorn.
Piercing the flesh, mighty fast!
This will come to pass.

Be still and be present,
Faith then assures,
that the heavenly
sent scent is near!
A heaven sent scent
grows from the flowers' release,
the journey
from the thorn to the petal,
soil at its feet.
The soil from all broken down
organic matter,
gives the rose its thorn-built ladder.

Only those willing to go,
to grow, will reach the reward,
of their faith
built heavenly cord, climbing up
the thorn
laden ladder!
Bear no mind, in this thorn matter.

The Pilgrimage continues along,
singing life's many songs.
One of faith and not of scorn,

will allow the Heart to build faith,
have hope, and love,
that which is to be born.
The life-string woven
of many a day,
now turned to a rope,
will allow one to cope,
and learn how to pray.

Now and forever, starting today.
Seeking wisdom and knowledge,
guidance,
in all of Gods' sources,
will give enlightenment to those,
daily challenging courses.

Some are of joy and others
with sorrow
and regret thorns,
all traveling roads
that may be lonely
and forlorn.
Never to fear or regret,
all is here to let us flex our faith
and build in our heart
for us to take part
in Wisdom's way to get
to our Heart!

So, start.
Open your Heart petals wide!
No longer a need to hide.
Release God's Heavenly sent scent.
Walk in Faith, giving Hope,
see what Love has sent
God's heart to yours, as a present!

Hello, Goodbye

Hello, goodbye.
A wave, a smile, and a cry.
The voice quivers,
as the life force shivers,
To release the final goodbyes.

Longing to stay,
Longing to go,
Longing for that forever home.
Yet, just not yet ready to roam,
into the ethereal places.

The one with bountiful graces,
as those we hold dear,
are earthly near.

Hear the celestial songs,
not so distant as they now
belong,
to the opening of the veil,
this soon to be the earth
to heaven's trail.

Notes sweetly heard close by,
relatives know the call and why!
Their Loved One is now
close to hearing the call,
Emotions arising in all.
Love to each and every one.

That's the totality, the full measure,
the journey well run.
Now, just before the final call,
Hugs, kisses, words of love,
and a bid adieu,
"I'll send my love back to you!
Oh, my soul, take me home!"
"Hello, goodbye now is the cry.

My breath leaving is my signal,
my Goodbye."
"Hello, now, my hearts sigh,

Reaching upward towards
the heavenly sky."

"Rejoice in my favor,
Forever savor,
Memories sweet.

Remember only those that love
gathers to your breast.
Let go of the rest!'
"My gift to you,
Our lives intertwined,
God put us all together at just
the right time!"

"So goodbye to you,
my dearest one,
No tears, just remember
our times of joy
and fun!
I now say hello in my new place,
my home.
No worries, just joy,
God's eternal grace.

I BELIEVE

I believe in the Goodness
of God,
His daily care.
His help for all of us "down there."
I believe in rainbows and
butterflies,
That aids in transforming
our lives.

I believe in Hummingbirds that
flitter about,
Give our souls joy, hope and
something to smile about.
I believe in Truth and Honesty.
No hiding in shadows, please.

I believe in beauty and art,
That which inspires and helps
us take
part in Life
Amid our strife.
I believe in the love of friends,

Those loyal through all, even
until our days on earth end.

I believe Angels assist us
if we ask and pray,
Protecting us night and day.
I believe in Life in giving gratitude.
Uplifting all in their attitudes.

I believe we each have
a wonderful part,
Destined from our birthed start.
One to fulfill God's plan.
That is to take a stand,
In righteousness in this Earth land.
I believe we can overcome,
Evil that seems rampant to some.

I believe!
Can you also be,
a believer with me?

IMAGINE A WORLD

Imagine a world of Peace, Love,
and Harmony.
One for all,
bonded,
a loving humanity.

Towards oneself
and others the
same,
The Golden Rule, etched
in one's heart,
bearing each other's
name.

The Living
in this life, becoming
the one sought direction,
Everyone desiring
to reach
this perfection!

Songs have been written and sung,
calling us to be ONE.
Feel it.
See it.
Be it.

The first rung in the
upward journey,
this ladder to joy,
embedded in these songs
that have been sung,
in each of us to be
at inner peace,
our inner song, inwardly sung.

Let us each start,
do our part.
Nothing else needs to done.
Except to enjoy life, being alive
with our inner harmony
and fun.

Imagine a world,
imagine and see,
Our world free,
of negativity.
Reverse the current
polarity.

Flip that inner switch,
find your
inner Peace nitch.

Become creative,
in one's
approach,
to allow this world
to be.

LOVE IS THE WAY

Angels came from Heaven
felt prayer,
pointing and protecting All
under God's care.

Multitudes of the
Heavenly Hosts,
(now, when all need
them the most)
to just one or two.
All Powerful and Loving
me and you.

God so desires
Peace on Earth.
Earth the place,
that He created and gave birth.

Children of every nation and race,
come along, hurry your pace,
free oneself from hate,
in one's mental place.

Get moving with God
and Angel grace.
Bring Harmony,
Peace,
Prosperity to all,
starting in your Heart space!

Angels to illumine
those that follow darkness trails,
From and in all,
countries/governments/media's
portraits
of the division they wish to impart.

Their money and schemes,
are now being seen.
So, follow the only true path,
the one that will
eternity last.
The trail and path of Love.

Follow God and his angels
from above!
Have strong faith,
see God's Angel signs!
Now come find
His Love's way!
Truth has been hidden
by evil's agendas
under dark veils.

Meow-Now Prayer!

All around,
we see the effects of the now.
Even the cats know how to
meow the now.
No future without
this meow-now.
The past no longer,
fading back
into the void,
taking a curtsy and a bow.

No matter how we desire to
control, to change the outcomes,
Good, awful, or just the total sum,
of that place in time,
time passes by, stopping
for no one!

We are blind!
Blinded by our desires
and emotions
so raw.
There is a place we can yet call,
to be able to see,
to perceive,
to release the past and its effects,
the whys and what nots,
blame, et. al.

That is the meow-now advice!
Turn all sorrows, joys, and strife,
Inward and upward, to the realm
of Life.
God and His Dominion, Peace,
and Forgiveness
does hear our prayers,
He sees our tears.

Connect within,
turn away from shame, hate,
and sin.
God feels our grief and feels
our pain,
wishing us all to regain,
our center and be free of this pain,
the place where our hearts have
been emotionally slain.

Know that the present,
the meow-now is the key!
Stay here to be near,
to be witness to God's inner call.
"You are my child, one and all."

Pray for those that are lost and
driven to evil's distraction.
Pray for strength and righteous
decisions and actions.
Pray unceasingly, help all be free.

So, all souls can worship beautifully!
Praying and being Love
to each other,
here on earth and for eternity.

My Friend

My friend, to the very end.
Through thick and thin.
We always win!

Joined together through
the bonds of love, friendship,
and grace,
we travel together, through time
and space,

Holding each other's hearts
in our hands, giving each other
a very sacred place.
A place to be delivered, to see,
we are loved and free!

Forever entwined by
love's plan divine,
we will forever be friends,
throughout eternity and time!

To our friendship, forever, I call you,
My Friend.
Do you hear my spiritual phone?
Calling you, My Friend?
Oh! How Dear you are,
my special Friend!

My Garden of Peace, My Garden of Love

My Garden of Peace,
My Garden of Love,
residing, not hiding,
out my back door with
the blue sky above.

This is a Paradise of Peace,
a quiet release,
a Sacred Space,
to rest and feel God's Grace.

Created to release all things
in Life
that have been weighted.
All things complicated.

A Worry-free Zone.
No room for cell phones!

Butterflies to flutter by,
Hummingbirds zooming
to the flowers
close by.
Each sending messages
of a spiritual tone.
Walking in and through the Garden
of Peace, the Garden of Love,
help me tarry along.

Now, leaving those former bits and
pieces of memories sown.
Releasing the seeds of thoughts
now gone and grown.
Other things that have taken
place long ago, need to be
released, to be let go.

Let these seeds of the past
now grow,
into Love and Peace.
Let them all be released!

Free of the complications of
thought provoked reasonings.
Sprinkled now with Wisdom,
Peace, and Love, as the Perfect
spiritual seasonings!

Let me walk in this Garden
of Peace and Love,
Playing with the hummingbirds
and Turtle Doves.

Let me see the Swallowtail
butterfly,
alight upon a flower nearby.

Let me feel your cool breeze
upon my face, Your Grace!

Let me hear the rustling
of the leaves,
if you please!

See the free birds in the air?
Take me there!

Oh, Garden of Peace and Love,
Give me your heavenly,
ever-lasting release!
Created for me, to return
to inner-mind peace!
Sown now with the seeds
of Peace and Love!

Northern Lights

Northern Lights
You are a delight!
Shine, oh, ever so bright!
Let us all see,
Your beauty!

On the Road Again

On the road again.
Will this road end?

Is it to our Home?
Or a journey to a place
that's awaiting our fate?
Is it a full circle or straight?
Curvy, with detours that
make us slow down and wait?

Destination known?
Unknown?
Is there a map, a course?
Or are you going on a whim?
Where does one really begin?

Do we drive, walk, bike, or
are we flying?
Are we smiling or is one

crying?
Laughing or grim?
Just begin!

Standing still, an option.
Forward or reverse?
Can be a blessing or a curse.

Best to check with the best
navigator known,
Wisdom learned from our
Spiritual Home.

Take time to explore,
Wisdom's advice and more.
Seek the advice of an
experienced traveler who has
traveled your course before.

Maybe they can help lessen
the blows,
the adverse footsteps,
as an experienced traveler
has already come to know,
there's a path that's a better
way to go!
So, on the Road again,
my friend,
be blessed mightily and
come to know,
wisdom and experience
are
two friends to help you go,
and grow,
fulfilling your Divine plan.

Once Written So

Once written so,
darkness has nowhere to go,
but into the light,
forever shining bright.

The Light of Love Divine,
for some, is harder to find.
Remember to always be kind.

Pain and angst have clouded
their way.
They forgot how to pray.

Awake now,
begin to climb!
Feel God's presence,
so sublime.

Always here, never there.
God cares!

Feel and breath this so.
There is really no other
place to go.

Sit, breath, be.
You will be this reality!

Oh, so bright,
this love light.

Embrace it to one's very core,
Let the past go,
no longer keeping score.
Be free and freer still.
Let this be your free will.

Once written upon one's
mind and heart,
now one may fully live and
take part,
of Life, of Love, and freer still,
that of an awakened free will.

Enlightenment, some may say,
it is just an awakened heart's way,
to birth one's soul's honesty,
to be steadfast and not sway.

Trusting in the possibilities,
of life as a beloved one's
journey back home,
one from which all left to
roam.

Some may need an
awakened one's touch,
to rewrite a path that
became twisted and lost.
One's soul now the Boss.

When one is ready, one now
can be spirit fed,
and led,
all in due course.
Love and Light never to
force.

Choose to come home, now,
that's all God desires.
He will never tire.
Awaiting one's soul
to be on fire.

Once written in stone for us
to see.
Now all that needs to be,
is a free will desire and
choice,
to hear and follow
God's voice.

ONE EYE

One Eye,
Is it open, is it closed?
Who knows.
Where does the vision go?

Blind? Single vision?
A decision?

Can we see with the single eye?
Dual vision, down to one?
Surely, it is no fun! Or is it better
to be "just One?"

Is the Spiritual Eye of being
"one", is it uniting, not dividing,
no longer duality as our reality?

Or is it more?
A gate to Heaven's door?

We can cope, we can have hope.
It is not the end of our rope.
One-eyed vision, for one eye
permanently closed is still sight,
in our fight, to remain whole.

The spiritually minded use the
meta- physical reminder, that
the One Eye of eternity is the
Spiritual Eye that frees us to
be no longer in an earth binder!

Take a deep breath, give out
a sigh, spiritualize your eye.
See deeply inside with
the uniting One Eye!

OUT OF THIS WORLD

Out of this world
journeys dwell.
Lifted up by dreams,
and balloons as well.

Float higher and higher still,
until,
one can clearly see, and be,
that astronaut floating above,
for all to see.

Floating amongst the stars,
and not very far,
are his cat friends, who see,
and want to be with him
on his journey.

Earth, Saturn, Jupiter, or Mars,
are all possibilities open to him,
so far.

One cat, floating on a magical
carpet ride,
the other cat inside,
the rocket where he can spy
and see,
all the wonders possible
for this boy
to enjoy and be.

So, wish upon a falling star,
wish to journey and go far,
far above perceived possibilities.

Go where no one else can dream
or be.
Journey to be, your highest
possibility.

We are each made to soar,
to roar,
with enthusiasm in life.
Rising above limitations and strife.

Shoot for those stars!
Go far,
in one's life.
Dream the impossible dream!
Beam yourself amongst the stars.
Be your own star!

PATHWAY OF HOPE

Loss and tragedy on this day,
also gave way for God,
to show and say everything
is and will be ok.

Surrounded in an Orb of Love,
A Pathway straight was seen,
leading the way to Heaven above.

The Orb in the beam of light,
surrounding loved ones who
lost their earthly life in this
tragedy plight.

Comfort now in the know,
as God in His infinite Wisdom
Love is showing all are forever
in His Love Light!

(Dedicated to Noble Fox
Artist's Grandson!
Artist: Yvonne Gidget Day
9-13-2022)

POETRY AND PROSE

Poetry and prose,
who knows where the thoughts
will go.
Weaving a tapestry of musings
and meanderings,
giving meaning to obvious and
at times to hidden things.

The art and beauty to reveal
is inherent in the writing,
style, and depth of emotions
to feel.

Where does the prose go?
Into the mind, then the soul?
Or do tell, does it cast a spell?
To entice one to look
deeper within?
Does the poetry help begin,
reflections,
directions,

anticipations,
heartfelt occasions?

Immediately or later?
To unravel a timetable?
Do the words open or close?
Do you see with your
eyes or through the prose?

Struggling, enticements,
stimulating excitements.
Depth beyond measure
giving deeper thought treasures?

Then it's worth, measurable
and pleasurable.
Bringing two sides together.
A coin to help join,
the height to the depth
allowing the precept to be one!
One with the profiteer,
one with the reader so dear!

Prayer for Life

We pray,
everyday!

Today,
we pray to say.

"Bring forth your Healing Graces,
to all parts of the World and
into our heart spaces."

Calm the inner griefs of war,
Give us your Love to help restore,
Our inner peace,
World peace.

Speed all healings brought to
our door,
From trauma induced
manifested actions and
more.

Send forth all Angelic aid into
this chaos and pain!
Send forth healing,
our hearts have need!
We need to be freed!

Free us from Evil's intent
and plans.
Let Love and Peace be where
we all can stand.

Safe, protected, loved ones, too.
Throughout the world,
Give each of us your
protection and Heavenly view.

See all as well, under your
protection and love,
thwarting the evil from your
Hand and Your love.

End all wars,
whether inner or outer—fear
and hate,
before they manifest
into something
more.

Change hearts and minds to find,
Peace in all lands,
show us how to love and be kind!

Let Love restore
Us and more.

Bring forgiveness and
restoration
in all places and destinations.

Life and Love forever more!
This is the prayer we
implore.

Thank You, Oh, Holy Grace!
Thank you from all heart spaces.

Shepherd Us in Amazing Grace

Shepherd us in Amazing Grace,
Lord help us to keep pace!

Show us the Divine way.
Help us to pray.

Walk beside us through
the valleys and streams,
it seems the world is tearing
us apart
at the seams.

Your rod and staff
of righteousness
needs to be seen amongst us!

Wield your sword of Power
and Might.
Re-ignite our fervor, our
spiritual sight.

Cut through the layers of
deceit and sin.
Free us,
let truth win!
Feed us from within.

Grace, Amazing Grace,
is where we wish to begin.
A gift from you to us,
What a gift given,
please rush!

Pastures have been laid bare.
Enemies surround us.
Yet your mercy helps us prepare,
the way of restoration,
in preparation for the promise of
You!

Many are now ready,
years past due!
Waiting on the message of You.
Our soul now restored,
we will soar.

Mercy, protection,
abundance, and more!
Love, wisdom, peace,
here and now,
we will open our heart door!

We hear you knocking,
we are ready to explore.

Fears previously held now
have fled.
You, Dear Lord, have
Shepherded and led
us through these evil times.
We believe.
We are restored.

Faith grows in the story of
our anointing oil,
pointing to Your presence
in our lives
and our affairs.

We are Grateful for Your love
and care!
May our hearts overflow
with love for us to bestow,
Love to both enemies
and friends.
May we all dwell in the end,
in your House of Love, Lord.

SING IT TO THE TREES

Sing it to the trees,
Please.
Heartfelt love and beauty.

Let the trees pass this on,
to the sky and beyond.

Feeling the precious nature
of music reaching the stars,
taking our mind and souls
far.
Far, far, farther along
with their beautiful song.

Tree roots send this sound
deep within, where it also belongs.

Deeply rooted in eternity.
Once played, the music will
forever be,
free.

A song eternal for the world
to be,
a better place for the playing
of thee.

The tree bark,
takes its part,
to nourish thee.
Reflecting the image of the
cello players' passion
expertly.

Images floating by with the
wind,
Let us live, let us all begin,
this song of life and love
sprouting from deep within!

The cellos, made from the
wood essence,
singing their joy for all who
hear and are present!

Catavina, a movement to feel,
to hear,
Open your heart along with
your inner ear.
Hear the call!
Be one with all.

Become the note
so to float,
Higher and higher,
become one to inspire!

Take Your Shoes Off at the Door

Take your shoes off at the door.
Come "hear" (here)
and "see" more!

Secure and multitudes of
options are already in store.
Freedom to pick and
choose galore!
An Irish phrase showing that
unbelievable expectations are
fulfilled and more!

Gee whiz, what bounty God
gives to us from His abundant
warehouse,
He is our Source, Come receive
His blessings from His Spiritual
store!

Be the new you!
Shake off the old dirt from those
old shoes!
God "has the stuff."
Believe me, He has more
than "enough."

Never to end, His Blessing pour
forth!
They flow endlessly, from the East,
West, South, or North! He Is our
Source!
Remember to tread lightly upon
the floor.

Come and be closer to God,
to see and hear more.
He exclaims, "You are dearer
than dear.
Let Me hold you near."
"Let me carry you, through the
dark times and into the Light,
In Me, you will find 'delight.'"

Hear His whisper to be free,
So let yourself be free!
Let us all be free, to love
unconditionally.
Free of the past, no longer to last.

"Home" is here. Come, be near!
In God you can go, to grow,
He is closer than you know!

Desperate the need was felt,
emotionally hitting one below
the belt!

Searching for what in the future
the desire wanted to be,
One not residing in "The God
Plan," not residing in THEE!

Shake off that dust and grim
from one's mental travels,
release those inner battles.
Safety is in HIS arms of Love!

Let go and surrender to God above!
Perfect control, as one knows,
comes freely and forever shows,
how God's Plan unfolds.

Jump off the cliff of doubt and fear,
God's safety net and Angels
will always be here.
Frets and worries age one so!
Needless are they, so let them all go!

Be a Joy bubble,
burst the fret and worry trouble!
Let the sunshine in! Grin!
And begin, a Joyful journey within.

So, let the dirty old shoes at the
mind's door, come with God,
and explore your new way
of life and more!

THE BOW TO THE STRING

Oh Violin, Violin, pull me
along with your song.
Straight to the bow,
to show me
the way to go.

Uplifting,
drifting,
into the beyond.
Sing your song.
Come along.

Lift me, lift me, lift me.
Oh, please let me see,
the heights of ecstasy,
of your joyful song.

Come along.
Bring others along,

with your song,
sing it sweetly,
sing it long!
Sing it softly, into the night,
Let your notes drift out of sight!

Oh, Violin, with your
Bow to the string,
it rings,
Nay, the strings joyously sing,
a tune that forever brings
One's soul to also sing.

Pull that bow across the string.
Let us begin
our song.
The one
we are meant to sing.
Our song, to carry us along!

THE DUFF

The *Duff*
is usually the opposite of buff.

Vernacular, for sure,
to bully those who
are "designated"
to receive a blow!

Designated ugly, fat friend!
Duff is the word trend.
Only a perspective in the end.
Other words, in other years,
preceded this "new term",
bringing many to tears.

These attempts to demean,
cycle throughout generations,
Until those who know,
elevate above the word blow!
The words are sent,
attempting to "hide," to conceal,
the bullies' fear of them is "real."

They "trend" and hide behind
a word disguise,
trying to compromise,
their lack of perceived inner
and outer appeal.
Usually from inner pain,
brokenness or shame.

They puff up their desire
for peer approval,
by flaunting an attitude
of superiority,
disguising their feelings
of inferiority.
In their eyes, is that someone
else is below their style.
But, only for a while.

They have yet to learn the
"Golden Rule."
Do for others what you wish to be
done for you!

So, their Puffiness,
leads others to duress,
to intimidate at best,
the object or person they
are trying to "best."

In God's good glory,
that is never the end
of "the story."
As balance will come into
"The Play"
as long as the Duff stands up
and chooses to display,
their commitment to say,
"I am OK.
I do not need your opinion
of me to matter."

"I am as worthy as you,
since this Duff title is only
your view!"
We are all the same irrespective
of a "word" game!

As throughout life. and strife,
we all are on the same field of play.
Whether we shine or are blind,
we each will have a turn to say,
"Today, I am the star,
by raising the bar!

Elevating those who grow,
to know,
God's children are we all."
So, just stand tall,
Give love to all,
that's how one wins the word game.

THE LOOK

The "Look"
is all it took,
to set straight
the message with the
intended fate!

Whether a look, a glance
of a woman's gait and prance,
from those that drive by,
with a twinkle and a wink
in their eye.

Another special look can be
found,
with our pet's eyes, looking
towards us, not making a
peep or sound.

The "Look" speaks loudly of
their intent,
come feed me, pet me,
give me your attention for the
love I've sent!

Other looks are a message,
urgency implied,
Here's what I spied!
Come quick, come see,
look what is beautiful to
share with me.

Sometimes, the "Look" is for
caring,
sometimes to stop the daring!
Over enthusiasm loosens
restraint,
Allows one to have inner
control before pain and faint.

The "Look" is to help one
reflect, to redirect,
to be open for cautionary
thinking to arrive,
before the daredevil event-dive.

Or a look from a parent
to a child to quell their rant,
Bringing harmony to their
home.

The child's soul now
to begin to roam,
a time for reflection,
for the child to learn
a better direction.

The "Look" has many a view,
many thoughts and emotions
to review,
look for another option that's new.

A "Look" of adoration,
one to help contemplation,
A "Look" of acceptance,
Approval, disapproval, and
many other emotional directions.

So, actions speak louder than
words,
We have all been told and
heard.

So, remember to send the "Look"
of acceptance, of love,
of peace from above.

The "Look" is here for each
of us to find,
a better way to be loving,
and kind.

TREE OF INSPIRATION

Tree of Inspiration,
growing about in our
very location.

Leaves sprout,
the Tree of Inspiration shouts,
"I am here, and many other
inspirational trees are all about."

"Come sit underneath me!
Come to be inspired, to see."

"Here, written by the wind,
washed by the rain,
ideas are imprinted on the leaves
for one to gain, an idea,
a quotation, or thoughts
maybe even for fortune and fame."

"Look up and see!"
"The tree limbs are supported
by me."

"Come up and sit here with me,"
invites the Inspiration Tree.

"With the sun,
come,
let's have some fun!"

"All comes together,
to make this endeavor
available for thee.
Take the time to be
free."
"Come, sit with me!"

"Free to indulge in the
inspirations that will
blossom."

"Come, hit that ideal home run."
"Use me,
feel me,"
invites the Inspiration Tree.

"Let your roots grow through me,"
suggests the Inspiration Tree.
 "Dig deep, grow wide,
allow ideas no longer to
hide!"

"Give life, give birth,
ideas have intrinsic worth!"
 "Send those ideas out in search,
of their need of life's expression,
of life's lessons, of their worth."

"Bare much fruit,
in pursuit,
of birthing these desires;
thoughts, that for many others,
could and should,
inspire!"

"Never grow tired."
Just get Inspired!"

"Sit, here below,
sit until you come to know,
that your will and desires,
which inspire, will climb
as you grow."

"Sprout, then sprint,
to the top of the tree!
There you can shout about it
and set your inspirations free!
Let this so be!"

"The seeds that have been inspired
from you in this tree.
Now, let the wind carry them.
Engaging fully in His Glories
and glorious occasions.
Intertwining,
no whining."

What God Wants is Our Love!

Our creativity in this pursuit.
To be One in the fun,
seeking Him and the Spirit
of Life,
to indwell in the deep well
of His creation.

Passion, in these endeavors.
Deeply experienced and felt.

So fixed in this expression,
mountains could fall and no one
would notice.
Or voice a displeasure or concern.

This enraptured state
is what the Sages and Saints voice
and celebrate.

The deepest of connection,
the one-sided direction
of Union.
This is the true communion!
The Lover's embrace,
the Spiritual embrace.

The emotions and eyes,
the heart, only spies,
This God embrace.

That is what God desires!
For us never to tire,
from the Spiritual embrace.
Enjoy this Union and Grace.

Take the time,
unwind,
be at peace,
release,

The world's distraction,
its constant hectic pace
and action!

Be The Love to God that He wants,
that HE desires.
Inspire,
You and others.

Wake us up to be more than
we can dream to be!
With You!
Anytime, anywhere!
That's what I want!

Where is my Love?

Oh, where is my love?
IS that you?
Come to me anew!
Touch me deeply inside,
That's where I hide!
Waiting for the breath, the sigh.

Love to awaken from the fears,
the pains.
That which kept me deep inside,
To hide.
Hide from what love seeks to gain.
Romeo and Juliet felt
this emotional
drain.

To be without love, there is
emotional pain,
the heart strains.

To be whole, to regain,
The love connection of the heart
and soul.
The love union of the soul flame.

Intertwined,
The feelings so sublime,
Music at times can only reveal,
Deeply what one feels.
The notes carry one away,
To the inner depths to say,
Fear, release your hold!

Pain melt away, release the load!
See the way,
Be the way,
For love to unfold.

The ecstasy, the reality,
the connection,
the direction,
of the spirit fully alive.

Engage in the rhythm,
yet there is more.
The connection to the essence,
the core.

Where is my love?
Here, there, below, above?
Outside? Inside?
Love now and always,
Here,
Come and be near!
Let's listen and hear,
The depth of love alive!

Once found,
The heart sounds,
The call to the place of love.
Cannot be fully described,
Only felt with the vibrating heart
strings, playing inside.

Once, where the fear
and pain dwelled,
Now gone, it's freed, the heart
grows and swells in the symphony
of life and love,
Shared with those who, too,
have no limits, no bounds,
Just becoming one being and
playing from the heart, love
sounds.

Who are You?

Who are you?
The Spirit asked.
Who are you, which
death has passed?
Who are you, that you are
still here?
Who are you,
oh, death was so near.

Reply, with a wink from one's eye.
"A blessed one," came the cry.
Prayers from those around,
Have kept one earth bound.
To aid in the journey
of another's plight.

Or, to help enlighten another
with God's wisdom and might.
Angels abound,
They are all around.

Waiting for a Prayer to sound.
Coming from our heart,
Or our lips,
Sometimes it's a thought
that slips.

Out and about,
To bring one to the fore,
Being here to help more.
Who are you?
Look deeper until
One knows their worth,
We are ordained from birth.
Receive the Love and
bring it into one's core.

There is plenty more,
all in store,
to find the answer to
"who are you?"

Do you know?
Do you show?

The Vessel of Love, the Light,
the glow?
Who are you?
One of God's own.

Angels to impart the wisdom
for us to grow,
And show God's love
that has been
sown,
Throughout Eternity.
Who are you?

Wings of Hope

One word, to set the Wings
of Hope,
afloat.
Flying higher and higher for
our souls to be,
Dedicated
to the Words and Wisdom
from God, for all to see.

The Power of dedication,
reverberating,
the celebration
of one's inner commitment
to truth.
Setting and sending one loose,
to experience,
to see,
the wisdom in dedicating to
a commitment,
to a wonderous cause,
or any event that makes the mind
and heart pause.

To be present, fully,
no absence in the direction.

Standing on the same side of
the fence,
the present.

This moment in time.
You will find,
all the answers within.
Now begin.
Dedicate this mental state.
Seal yourself in a dedicated
stance,
before time runs out,
before it's too late.

God and angels all waiting
for thee,
opening the fence door to
help set us free!

The dedication, from within,
is to begin,
the journey.

The pace,
not a race,
is bringing truth for us to face,
all that is real, rewarding,
restoring, and glorifying
us as God's chosen race.

Fly on the Wings of this
Hope,
dedicate oneself to this
current of Love.

Fly higher and higher,
dedicated to this noble
pursuit.

Continue against all odds.
This is the seal of approval,
God's homeward nod.
Dedicating, body, mind, and soul,
to the One and only Worthy goal.

The inner renewal of our Soul.

You are NOT a Princess

You are not a Princess.
You are nothing less
than the QUEEN!
And you need to be seen.

About the Author

Dr. Teresa Quinlin was uniquely gifted from birth with talent and insight that is reflected in her life today. The daughter of Tom and La Donna Quinlin, she was raised in Minster, Ohio. She attended the College of St. Joseph in Cincinnati and Wright State University Medical School specializing in Family Practice. In her Canal Winchester, Ohio, practice she specializes in wellness with complimentary modalities including acupuncture and other natural approaches. Her primary goal is to be instrumental in providing the best health options for all her patients.

www.ingramcontent.com/pod-product-compliance
Lightning Source LLC
LaVergne TN
LVHW021505080426
835509LV00018B/2405